DATE DUE

This is a Let's-Read-and-Find-Out Science Book™

Sunshine Makes the Seasons

REVISED EDITION

by Franklyn M. Branley · illustrated by Giulio Maestro

Thomas Y. Crowell   New York

Other Recent Let's-Read-and-Find-Out Science Books™ You Will Enjoy

Hurricane Watch · What Happens to a Hamburger · My Visit to the Dinosaurs
Flash, Crash, Rumble, and Roll · Dinosaurs Are Different · Volcanoes · Germs Make Me Sick!
Meet the Computer · How to Talk to Your Computer · Rock Collecting
Is There Life in Outer Space? · Comets · All Kinds of Feet · Rain and Hail
Why I Cough, Sneeze, Shiver, Hiccup, & Yawn · You Can't Make a Move Without Your Muscles
The Sky Is Full of Stars · The Planets in Our Solar System · Digging Up Dinosaurs
No Measles, No Mumps for Me · When Birds Change Their Feathers · Birds Are Flying
A Jellyfish Is Not a Fish · Cactus in the Desert · Me and My Family Tree
Redwoods Are the Tallest Trees in the World · Shells Are Skeletons · Caves
Wild and Woolly Mammoths · The March of the Lemmings · Corals
Energy from the Sun · Corn Is Maize

The *Let's-Read-and-Find-Out Science Book* series was originated by Dr. Franklyn M. Branley, Astronomer Emeritus and former Chairman of The American Museum-Hayden Planetarium, and was formerly co-edited by him and Dr. Roma Gans, Professor Emeritus of Childhood Education, Teachers College, Columbia University. For a complete catalog of Let's-Read-and-Find Out Science Books, write to Thomas Y. Crowell Junior Books, 10 East 53rd Street, New York, NY 10022.

Sunshine Makes the Seasons
Text copyright © 1974, 1985 by Franklyn M. Branley
Illustrations copyright © 1985 by Giulio Maestro
All rights reserved. No part of this book may be used or
reproduced in any manner whatsoever without written permission
except in the case of brief quotations embodied in critical
articles and reviews. Printed in the United States of America.
For information address Thomas Y. Crowell Junior Books,
10 East 53rd Street, New York, N.Y. 10022.
Published simultaneously in
Canada by Fitzhenry & Whiteside Limited, Toronto.
10 9 8 7 6 5 4 3 2 1
Revised Edition

Library of Congress Cataloging in Publication Data
Branley, Franklyn Mansfield, 1915–
    Sunshine makes the seasons.

    (Let's-read-and-find-out science book)
    Summary: Describes how sunshine and the tilt of the
earth's axis are responsible for the changing seasons.
    1. Seasons—Juvenile literature. 2. Sunshine—Juvenile
literature. [1. Seasons] I. Maestro, Giulio, ill.
II. Title. III. Series.
QB631.B73 1985b   525′.5   85-47540
ISBN 0-690-04481-X
ISBN 0-690-04482-8 (lib. bdg.)

    (A Let's-read-and-find-out book)
    "A Harper trophy book."
    ISBN 0-06-445019-8 (pbk.)   85-42750

Sunshine warms the earth.

If the sun stopped shining, the earth would get colder and colder. We would freeze. The whole earth would freeze.

The sun shines all through the year. But we are warmer in summer than in winter. The amount of sunshine makes the difference.

The earth spins around, or rotates, once in twenty-four hours. That's why we have day and night. When we are on the sun side of the earth, there is daylight. As the earth rotates, we turn away from the sun. There is sunset and then night.

At the same time that the earth spins, it goes around the sun. The earth takes a year to make one trip around the sun.

During a year the length of our day changes. In winter the days are short. It may be dark by the time you get home from school. It is cold because we don't get many hours of sunshine.

As we move into spring, days become a bit longer. By summer they are even longer.

The days may be so long that it is still light when you go to bed. It is warm because we get many hours of sunshine.

After the long days of summer, the days begin to get shorter and cooler. It is fall and time to go back to school.

All through the year the earth has been rotating
once in twenty-four hours, giving us day and night.
And all through the year the lengths of darkness
and daylight have been changing. The seasons have
been changing too.

You can see the reason for these changes by using an orange for the earth, a pencil, and a flashlight. Push a pencil through an orange from top to bottom. The top is the North Pole. You can mark it with an N. The bottom is the South Pole. Using a marking pen, draw a line around the orange halfway between the poles. That's the equator. Stick a pin in the orange about halfway between the equator and the North Pole. Imagine this is where you live.

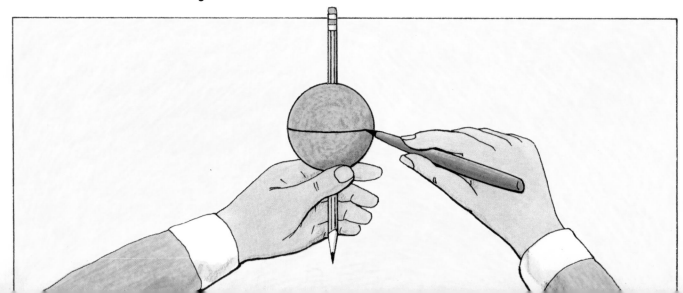

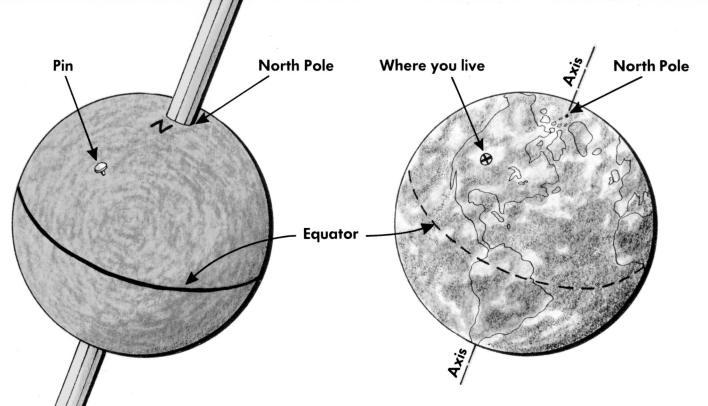

Pin · North Pole · Where you live · Axis · North Pole · Equator · Axis

Turn the pencil and the orange. The pencil is the axis of the orange.

The earth also has an axis. There is nothing like a pencil through the earth. But the earth spins as though there were something like a pencil running from pole to pole.

Hold the axis of the orange straight up and down. In a darkened room, have someone shine a flashlight on the orange.

The light is supposed to be the sun. The part of the orange toward the flashlight is in daylight. The other half is in darkness.

Daylight falls on the North Pole and also the South Pole, even when you spin the orange.

Walk all around the flashlight. Keep the light shining on the orange. That would be the same as the earth going all around the sun. It would be a year. Keep the axis straight up and down.

Wherever you are as you circle the flashlight, the orange is lighted from pole to pole. All through the year and all over the earth, days and nights would be the same length. There would be no change in seasons.

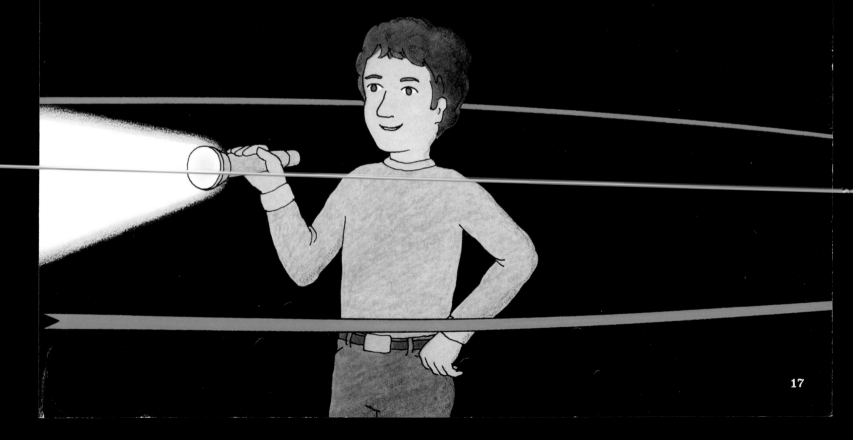

But we know that does not happen on the earth. The days get shorter and then longer as the earth goes around the sun. And winter changes to summer. It's because the axis of the earth is not straight up and down. It is tilted.

Let's experiment with the orange. This time tilt
the axis the way it is tilted in the picture. That's the
way the earth's axis is tilted. Hold the orange so the
North Pole is tilted away from the flashlight.

Turn the orange all the way around, and you will see that the pin is in the light only a short time. The northern half of the earth has short days and long nights. Sunlight does not fall on the North Pole. The North Pole has its long winter night. It is winter and it is cold.

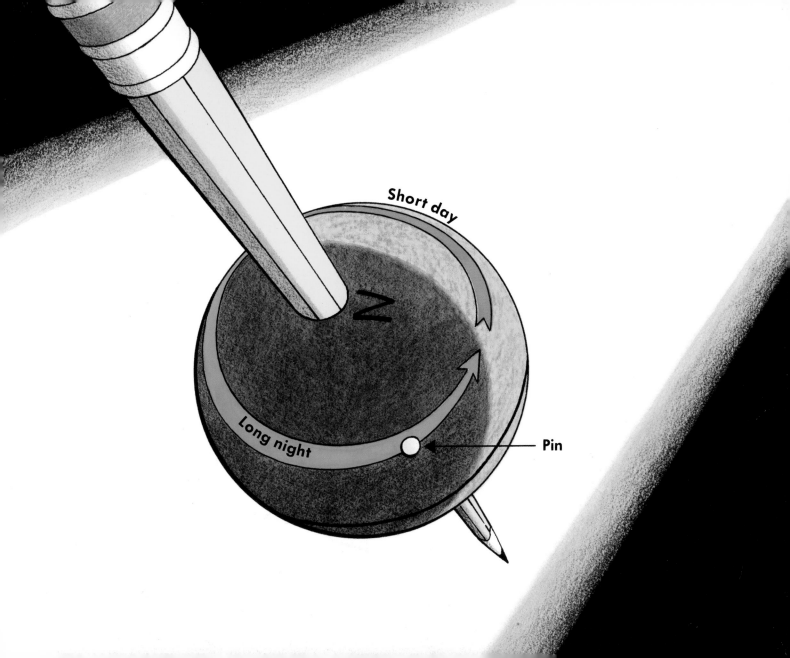

Keep the axis of the orange tilted in the same direction and go partway around the flashlight. Now the light falls on both poles. It is springtime in the north. Days are getting longer.

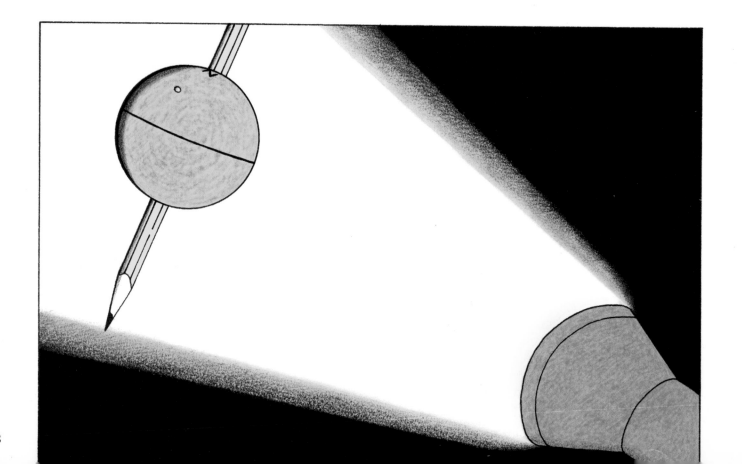

Without changing the tilt of the axis, move until you are halfway around the flashlight from where you started. Soon the North Pole will be tilted toward the light. It is summer.

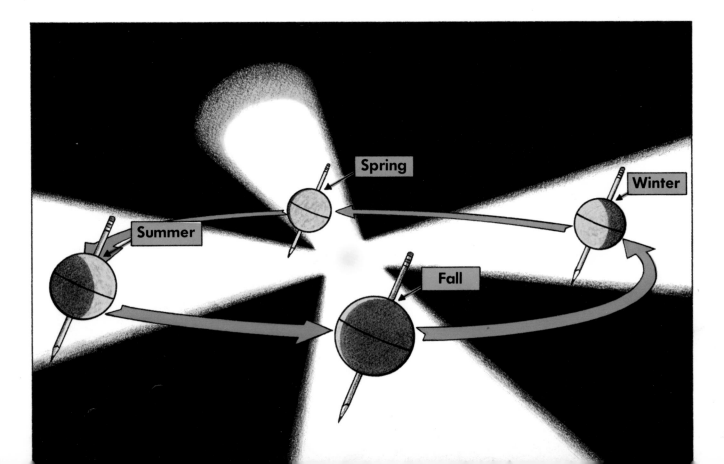

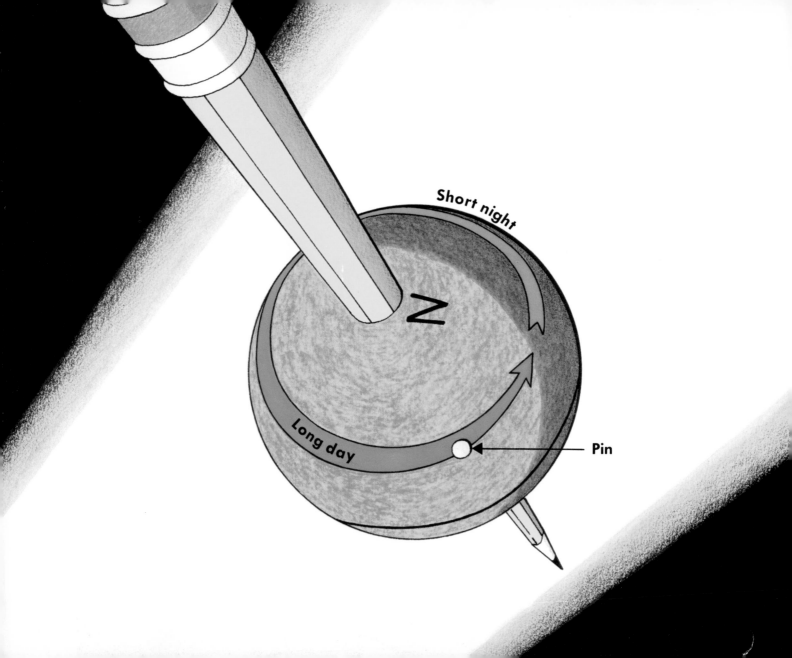

As you turn the orange, the pin is in the light longer than it is in the dark. The northern half of the earth has long days and short nights. The North Pole has its long summer day. It is summer and it is warm.

Keep moving around the flashlight. Remember, always keep the orange tilted in the same direction. You'll see that once again light falls on both the North Pole and the South Pole of the orange. It is fall in the north. The days are getting shorter, and cooler too.

Keep moving around and you come back to winter.

Winter   Spring   Summer   Fall

They happen because sunshine makes the seasons, and because the axis of the earth is tilted.

The southern half of the earth has seasons too. They are the opposites of our seasons. When it is summer and we are going to the beach, people on the southern half of the earth have winter. They are skating and skiing.

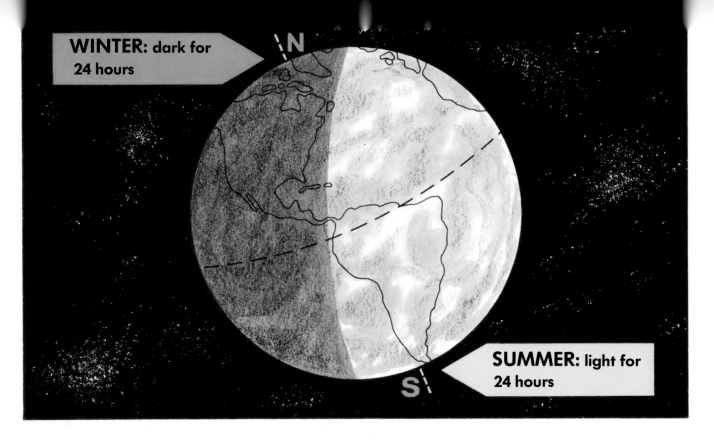

WINTER: dark for 24 hours

SUMMER: light for 24 hours

The North Pole and the South Pole also have seasons. Their winters are cold and dark. The sun does not rise every day. It is dark all winter long.

During summer at the poles, the sun does not set every day. For several weeks there is no night.

Seasons at the Poles are opposite. When the North Pole has winter, the South Pole has summer. Six months later, when it is winter at the South Pole, it is summer at the North Pole.

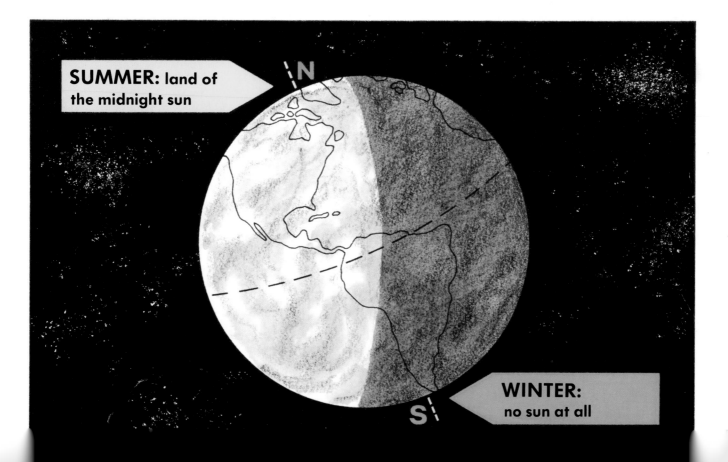

Along the equator it is warm all the time.
The temperature stays about the same all through
the year. You can see why if you experiment with
the orange. Move the pin to the equator.

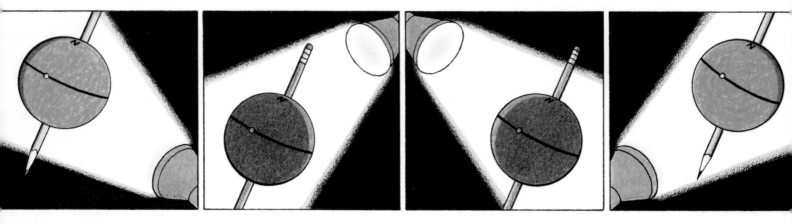

Watch the pin to see what happens as you go
through a year. You'll see that day and night are
just about the same length in summer and winter,
spring and fall.

That's good if you like warm weather all the time. But it's also nice to see snow once in a while, to see the flowers and birds of springtime, to go swimming in summer, and have pumpkins in the fall.

Year after year the days change, and so do the seasons. We have winter, spring, summer, and fall because the sun warms the earth. And because the axis of the earth is tilted.